THE HUMAN BODY

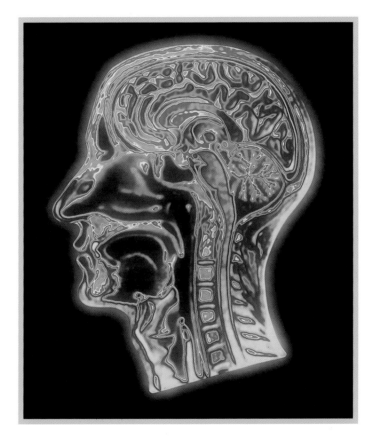

by
John Farndon

***B*ENCHMARK *B*OOKS**

MARSHALL CAVENDISH
NEW YORK

Marshall Cavendish Corporation

99 White Plains Road

Tarrytown, New York 10591

© Marshall Cavendish Corporation, 2002

Created by Brown Partworks Ltd

Library of Congress Cataloging-in-Publication Data

Farndon, John.
     The Human Body / by John Farndon.
            p. cm. – (Science experiments)
Includes index.
ISBN 0-7614-1339-1
     1.Human physiology—Experiments—Juvenile literature. [1. Body, Human. 2.
     Human physiology. 3. Human anatomy.] I. Title.

P42.F375 2001
612'0078—dc21   2001025214

Printed in Hong Kong

PHOTOGRAPHIC CREDITS

t – top; b – bottom; c – center; l – left; r – right

Corbis - p4,5 Jim Zuckerman (b); p10, Mike King (br); p20, Reuters New
Media Inc. (bl); p24,25 Jerome Prevost (b); p27, Daniel Geller (br)
Kobal Collection - p5, (tr)
Science Photo Library - title page, (c); p6,7 (b); p11 (tr); p22,23 (b); p23,
(tr); p26, (br)
Pictor International - p16,17 (b); p25, (cr)

Step-by-step photography throughout: Martin Norris

Front cover: Martin Norris

Contents

BODY BUILDING

Human bodies come in all shapes and sizes. Some people are tall, while others are short. Some people are fat and some are thin. But all human bodies contain the same basic parts and work in the same way.

Just like every other living organism in the world, humans are made entirely from tiny living units called cells. These are the building blocks of the body. Most living cells are so small you can only see them under a very powerful microscope. More than ten thousand of them would fit onto a pinhead.

Very simple life-forms, such as bacteria, are made from just a single tiny cell. The human body, however, contains more than 75 trillion cells.

Human body cells come in 200 or so different shapes and sizes. Each type of cell has its own special task. Red blood cells carry oxygen around the body. Skin cells make a protective outer layer. Fat cells provide an emergency energy store and also help to keep the body warm. Some parts of the body are made almost entirely

This powerful microscope photograph shows how a layer of skin is built up from individual body cells.

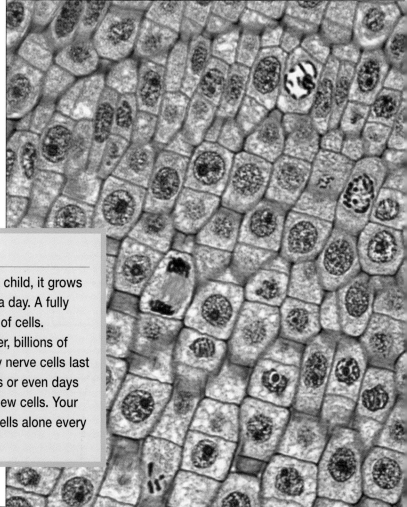

Did you know?

As your body develops when you are a child, it grows mainly by adding millions of new cells a day. A fully grown body is made of tens of trillions of cells.
But even though it then grows no bigger, billions of new cells are still made every day. Only nerve cells last all your life. Most cells last only months or even days and are constantly being replaced by new cells. Your body produces 200 billion new blood cells alone every single day!

from one kind of cell. The brain, for example, is made only of special nerve cells. Other body parts, such as the heart, are built up from a wide range of different cells.

Body cells are surrounded by a thin wall called a membrane. The membrane is thin enough to let certain chemicals pass in and out. It holds a watery fluid, or cytoplasm. At the heart of each cell is its nucleus, containing the chemical DNA. DNA provides all the instructions for the cell to

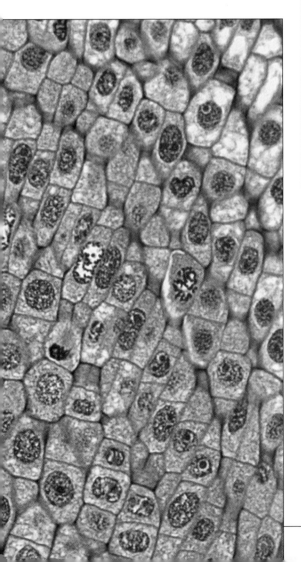

In the real world

ARTIFICIAL BODIES

The body is just billions of tiny cells stuck together, but what these cells create by working together is far beyond any machine. People have made lifelike statues for thousands of years. Medics make effective prosthetics (artificial replacements) for people who have lost body parts such as arms and legs. Scientists hope to create "virtual" people on computer. Others are trying to make thinking robots. But the idea of an artificial working human—an android—remains science fiction.

The creation of an android, such as Data from Star Trek, *is still sheer fantasy.*

operate. It also has instructions, passed on from parents, to build the entire body.

Cells group together to make tissues. There are four main kinds of tissues. Nerve tissue sends messages around the body. Epithelial tissue is elastic and waterproof and makes your skin and the walls of internal structures. Muscle tissue allows the body to move. Connective tissue, including bone, holds the body together.

ORGANS & SYSTEMS

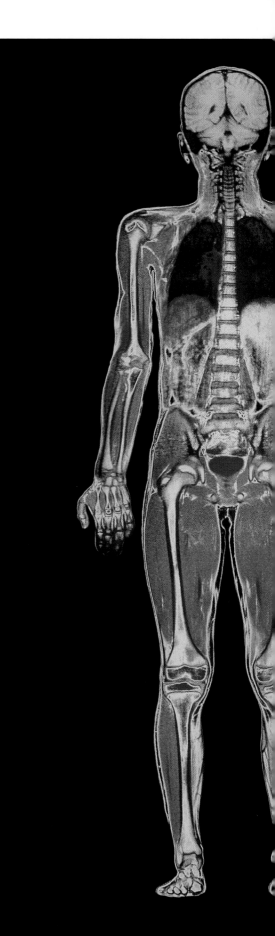

An ordinary home has certain places for certain tasks, such as a kitchen for making food and a bathroom for washing. The body also has special places for carrying out certain tasks. These places are called organs, and they are built up from tissues. The heart, for example, is the organ that pumps blood around your body. The kidneys are fist-sized organs in the lower back that filter waste water.

The size and shape of the organ depends on what it does. The organs inside the middle of the body, such as the heart, liver, and kidney deal with blood. They are jellylike lumps. The brain is the organ that fills

Photos of organs in a living body can be made using magnetic reflections from atoms. This is called an MRI scan. This MRI scan of a 9-year-old boy shows parts of major body systems, including the brain (orange), lungs (dark red), and liver (yellow).

Did you know?

Whether you are a girl or a boy, most of your body systems work in exactly the same way. The reproductive systems, however, are different. This system enables people to have children. It includes the sex organs and the chemicals that control them. The reproductive system is also the only system that can be surgically removed from a person's body without threatening his or her life.

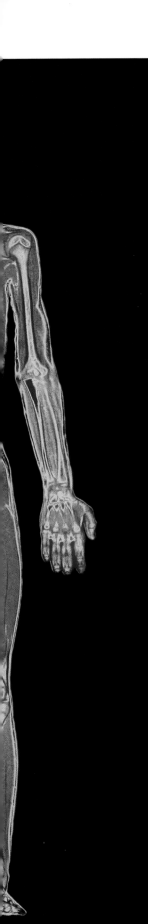

In focus

BODY SYSTEMS

All your body systems interact with one another, and, so, the distinctions between one system and another may not be clear-cut. These are some of the major systems.

- Skeleton, or skeletal system
- Musculature, or muscle system
- Cardiovascular system—the heart and blood
- Nervous system—the brain, spinal cord, and the nerves
- Digestive system—the mouth, stomach, intestine, and liver
- Immune system—the body's defenses against disease and injury
- Lymphatic system—lymph tubes that circulate lymph fluid containing cells that fight disease
- Excretory system—retrieves water from digested food and gets rid of solid waste
- Urinary system—controls the body's water content and removes excess as urine
- Respiratory (breathing) system, including the lungs
- Reproductive system—the special organs and controls that enable people to have children

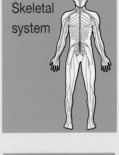

Skeletal system

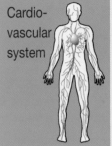

Cardio-vascular system

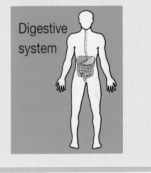

Digestive system

the head. It contains a dense mass of nerve cells to perform its complex task of controlling the body. The largest organ in the body is the skin.

The organs of the body rarely work alone. They are usually linked with other organs, tissues, and body cells. Pumps, pipes, boilers, and radiators work together to warm a house.

Like these, the organs, tissues, and cells in a body system work together to perform a task.

Some systems, such as the nervous system, extend through the whole body. Others are local, or confined to one area. The digestive system, which breaks down food, and the urinary system, which controls waste water are both local systems.

BREATH OF LIFE

You will need

- ✔ An empty plastic water bottle with a fitted nozzle
- ✔ Two balloons
- ✔ Scissors

1 Carefully cut the top third off an empty plastic water bottle, keeping the cut as straight as possible.

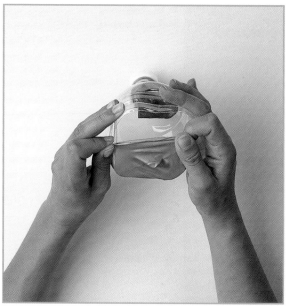

3 Cut the neck off the other balloon and stretch it tightly over the cut-off bottom of the bottle top.

What is happening?

In this project, the orange balloon is one of the lungs and the bottle is the chest cavity. The green balloon is the diaphragm, the sheet of muscle across the bottom of the chest that makes you breathe in and out. When the diaphragm is relaxed, it is curved upward, and your lungs empty (breathing out). When it pulls flat, it lowers pressure in the chest and inflates the lungs. As the lungs inflate, they draw air in (breathing in).

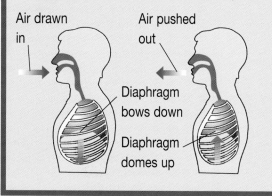

Air drawn in

Air pushed out

Diaphragm bows down

Diaphragm domes up

Did you know?

- There are about 300 million air sacs in your lungs.
- Opened out and laid flat, the inside of the air sacs would cover the area of an entire tennis court.
- Lungs have over 1,500 miles (2,400 km) of airways.

2 Slip one balloon over the bottle's nozzle and push the balloon (upside down) into the bottle neck.

You have now made a small model of your lung. Check that the nozzle is pushed right into the bottle neck, then grip the bottle neck firmly in one hand. Now pinch a bit of the balloon that is stretched over the bottom of the bottle between the finger and thumb of your other hand. Pull down on the stretched balloon while you look at the balloon inside the bottle. Pull as swiftly and firmly and as far as you can without pulling the stretched balloon off the bottle. Slowly release the balloon then pull it out again. You will notice that every time you pull on the stretched balloon, the balloon inside the bottle slightly inflates.

BREATHING AND BLOOD

To stay alive, every cell in your body needs a constant supply of oxygen. Oxygen is a gas that makes up 21 percent of the air around you. Your body gets it by inhaling. If you stopped breathing for even a few minutes, the body cells would be starved of oxygen and would start to die.

Air gets into your body through your lungs, two spongy

Whenever the body works hard, the muscle cells need extra oxygen. Runners breathe harder than usual, and their heart pumps faster.

Did you know?

There are over 40,000 miles (60,000 km) of tiny blood vessels in your body—yet, amazingly, all your blood circulates through them once every 90 seconds. It races through the widest blood vessels (arteries and veins) at over three feet (1 m) a second.

bags inside your chest. When you breathe in, air is sucked through your nose or mouth and down into your windpipe (or trachea) until it reaches a fork inside your chest. At the fork, the airways branch in two. One branch (or bronchus) leads to the left lung; the other branch leads to the right lung.

Inside each lung, the bronchus branches into millions of tiny airways, or bronchioles. Each bronchiole ends in tiny grapelike bunches of air sacs called alveoli (singular is alveolus). The walls of each sac are so thin that oxygen can seep through into the tiny blood vessels (tubes) wrapped around them. There are so many alveoli that the lungs can absorb huge amounts of oxygen from the air in just a few seconds.

Once oxygen is in the blood, it must be taken swiftly to body cells. At the same time, carbon dioxide—the waste gas from the cells—must be collected and brought back to the lungs for breathing out. This is why your heart circulates blood continually around your body.

The heart is the tireless pump inside your chest. It pushes oxygen-rich blood out around the body through blood vessels called arteries. Then it pulls the blood, without its oxygen, back to the lungs through blood vessels called veins.

In focus

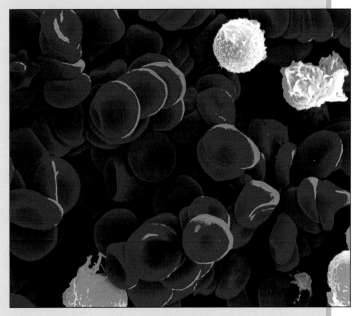

This microscopic view of blood shows it is packed with tiny red blood cells. It is these which give blood its color and carry oxygen from the lungs to body cells.

WHAT IS BLOOD?

Blood is the body's transport system. It not only carries oxygen from the lungs to every body cell, it also supplies the cells with food and takes away waste products. Blood helps spread heat, too, and plays a vital role in defending the body against disease.

Although blood looks like red ink, it is a mix of microscopic cells held in a yellowish fluid, called plasma. The red color comes from billions of tiny button-shaped red cells. The red cells carry oxygen from the lungs. The oxygen is held in the cells by a special chemical called hemoglobin. Hemoglobin is bright red when it is carrying oxygen but fades to purple when the oxygen is gone. As well as the red blood cells, the blood contains a complex range of larger white cells that help defend the body against germs. Finally, there are tiny lumps, called platelets, that allow blood to clot, or to plug wounds.

PULSE AND HEARTBEAT

You will need

- ✔ A length of plastic tubing about 3 ft (1 m) long and wide enough to fit over the neck of funnel
- ✔ A clock with a second hand
- ✔ A clean plastic funnel

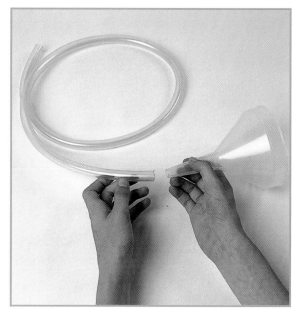

1 To listen to your heart, make a listening device by inserting a funnel into the end of a length of plastic tube.

In focus

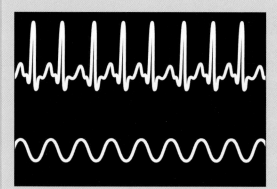

Heartbeat can be monitored and recorded by an electrocardiographic (ECG) machine. This registers tiny electrical impulses created by the heartbeat. The pattern should be even and regular.

HEART RATE

The heart pumps about a cupful of blood around your body every second. A normal child's heart beats (pumps) about 85 times a minute. An adult's heart beats more slowly, about 71 times for a man and 80 times for a woman. Vigorous exercise can increase the heart rate dramatically—especially in someone who is not fit. This is because the heart has to pump faster to keep the muscles supplied with oxygen. A heart rate of over 100 is called tachycardia. People who experience tachycardia when they are not exercising may have heart disease and should get advice from their doctor.

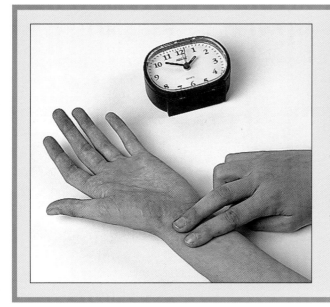

Gently lay two fingertips on the inside of your wrist in the slight dip on the thumb side. This is where a main artery nears the surface. Move your fingertips until you can feel a slight vibration. This is your pulse, the shock that runs through your blood when your heart pumps. Using a clock with a second hand, count how many pulses there are in a minute.

Place the mouth of the funnel against the middle of your chest, slightly to the left. This is where your heart is. Now place the other end of the tube in your ear, and listen hard. You should be able to hear your heart pounding. Run in place and you will hear your heart beat faster.

What is happening?

Your heart is a pump made from two muscular bags that contract every second or so to squeeze blood through the arteries. In between each squeeze, blood fills up the bag behind little flaps or valves. The sound you are hearing is the valves snapping shut and your blood moving through the arteries.

FITNESS

You will need

✔ Suitable clothes for running

✔ A clock or watch with a second hand

✔ A thermometer

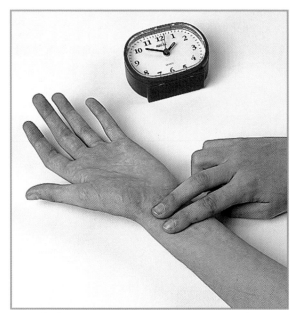

2 Get ready for a run, but, before you start, measure your temperature and your pulse.

1 Before you start, measure your pulse in the way described on page 13, while sitting down.

Now try this

Try measuring your temperature and pulse and checking other signs at intervals after you have stopped running. If you are fit, all your body systems should return to normal within a few minutes of a gentle run. After a long, hard run, however, it can take hours for your body to return to normal. This is because lactic acid—a waste product created by muscle activity—builds up in the muscles, and your body has to break it down and get rid of it. If you exercise regularly, you will find that your heart rate gets higher during exercise but goes back to normal more quickly when you stop exercising.

You can measure your blood temperature by holding a clean, disinfected thermometer under your tongue for one to two minutes.

3 Run hard and fast for at least ten minutes.

4 As soon as you stop running, measure your temperature and pulse.

FUELING THE BODY

Without fuel to keep it going, your body would soon stop working. This is the main reason why we eat. Food is the body's principal source of energy.

Body fuel comes from two basic kinds of food substances—carbohydrates and fats. Carbohydrates are sugars such as glucose, sucrose, and starch. They are found in foods such as bread, rice, potatoes, fruits, and cookies. Fats are greasy foods that will not dissolve in water. Some are solid, such as butter, meat fat, and cheese. Others are liquid, such as olive oil. The body does not usually burn fat up immediately. It stores it in cells around the body until it is needed.

Food also provides other vital materials, including proteins, fiber, and vitamins and minerals (see the box on page 17). Proteins make and repair cells. Meat and fish are high in protein, as are eggs, milk, and cheese. Fiber comes from plant fibers that the body cannot digest. Fiber keeps the digestive system healthy.

All these foods are carried in the blood to the body cells in the form of small simple molecules. The food you eat, however, comes in big lumps and liquids made from large, complex molecules. So, your body has a food processing system, called the digestive system, to break the food down.

The digestive system is a long tube that winds through the body. It starts with the mouth, runs down through your esophagus and into your stomach. It then

Your diet is what you eat. To stay fit, your diet must have the right amount of proteins, carbohydrates, fats and vitamins.

winds through long tubes called your intestines before finally ending at your anus.

As food passes through the digestive system, it is broken down physically by the pummelling it gets from the tubes' muscular walls, and chemically by acids and chemicals called enzymes. Eventually, it is in molecules small enough to be absorbed through the intestinal wall into the blood. From there, it travels to the liver to be distributed to the body cells.

In focus

DIGESTING FOOD

Digestion begins in the mouth, where food is softened by chewing, and by enzymes in saliva. But the main demolition yard is the stomach, which stretches as it fills with food. By the time food leaves the stomach, it has been churned up and dissolved into a semi-liquid mass, called chyme. From the stomach, chyme goes into the narrow first part of the intestine— the small intestine, where it is digested and absorbed into the blood. Any food not digested goes on into the large intestine ,where it is dried out and prepared for release through the anus.

The intestine has to be very long to perform its task, so it is folded over again and again inside your body. If you stretched it out straight, its length would be about five times your height.

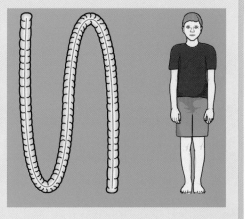

DIGESTION

You will need

- ✔ Some laundry detergent with and without enzymes
- ✔ Two strips of white cotton
- ✔ Four small dishes and a measuring cup
- ✔ Iodine
- ✔ A teaspoon and glass
- ✔ Some crackers
- ✔ Jam

What is happening?

Crackers are rich in starch, which is a type of carbohydrate. Starch turns iodine purple. When you drop iodine on a cracker, the iodine turns purple, showing the cracker contains starch. But the iodine does not turn the sucked cracker purple. This shows that digestion has already started, as the chemicals in saliva have dissolved the starch.

Iodine turns purple with the starch in the dry cracker (left) but has no effect on the sucked cracker (right).

1 Put a drop of iodine in a glass of water. Put a dry cracker in each of two dishes. Drop a little iodine on one cracker.

2 Suck the cracker with no iodine for a while. Return it to the dish and drop iodine on it.

1 Smear jam on the end of cotton strips. Mix each detergent in separate dishes with equal amounts of water.

2 Dip the end with jam of one cotton strip into the dish of detergent with enzymes and the other into the one without.

Leave the cotton strips to soak for about 30 minutes, then carefully lift them out. You should find that the strip that has been dipped into the detergent with enzymes is slightly less stained with jam than the strip dipped into ordinary powder. This is because jam contains a tiny amount of protein. Enzymes in your body are organic chemicals that break up proteins in your stomach. In the same way, the enzymes in the laundry detergent help break up the proteins in the jam.

WATER IN THE BODY

You will need

- A clear plastic bag (big enough to put your hand inside)
- Adhesive tape

What is happening?

Sweat is salty water that oozes from tiny pores in your skin called sweat glands. As sweat evaporates on the skin, it draws heat from the body. The evaporation cools the body down. That is why people sweat more when they exercise.

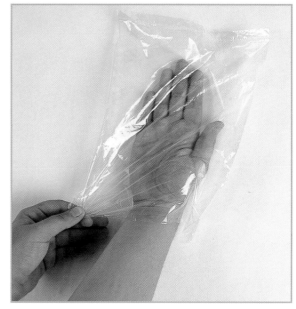

1 Slip your left hand inside a plastic bag (your right , if you are left-handed). Pull up the bag beyond your wrist.

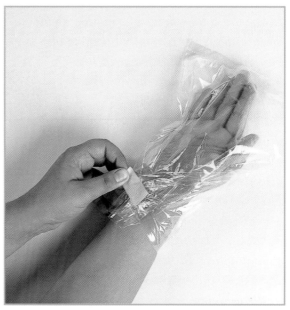

2 Fold the top edges of the bag tightly around your wrist. Now tape the edges together to make sure no air gets in.

Now try this

Blow on your finger. You feel the air blowing over it, but because your breath is quite warm, it does not feel cold. Now lick your finger and blow over it again. Suddenly, the breath seems like a chill wind. Why? Your breath has become no colder, but the moisture on your finger is evaporating—changing from a liquid to a gas. Evaporation requires heat, and the heat comes from your finger, which is why your finger suddenly feels cold.

Lick your finger wet, then try blowing on it. You will find it suddenly feels chilled.

After a while, the inside of the bag starts to steam up. The longer you leave it, the more it will steam up. Eventually, drops of water will form on the inside of the bag. This water is sweat coming out of the skin of your hand. Skin is producing sweat most of the time, but it normally stays dry, because the sweat evaporates into the air. The moisture that evaporates from your hand cannot escape from the bag, so it condenses (turns back to liquid) on the inside of the bag.

BARE BONES

If you did not have bones, your body would flop like jelly. Bones link together to make a strong framework called the skeleton. The skeleton provides an anchor for all the muscles. It also supports the skin and other tissues and protects the brain, heart, and other organs.

Altogether, your skeleton has about 200 bones, held together by rubbery cartilage. When you were a baby, your skeleton had 300 bones, but some bones fuse together as you grow. The skull, for example, begins as separate plates. The plates slowly fuse together into a single cap that encases the head.

This is a still from an animation of a skeleton, designed to show how all the joints move.

Did you know?

Bones are so strong that they can be squeezed twice as hard as granite and stretched four times as far as concrete without breaking. Yet, they are so light that they only make up 14 percent of your body's total weight. Weight for weight, bone is five times stronger than steel.

LIVING BONES

The bones of a skeleton look hard and dry, but while you are alive, your bones are living active tissues. In the core of each bone is a soft, jellylike tissue called marrow. This can be red or yellow, depending on whether it has more blood or fat. The red marrow of flat bones like the breastbone, ribs, shoulders, and hips are factories for new blood cells. Millions are made every second! Yellow marrow normally stores fat, but may turn red to make extra blood cells to help your body fight off illness.

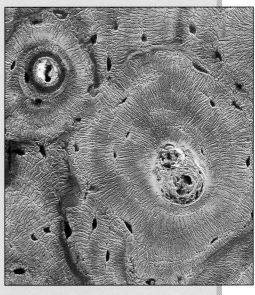

This microscope photograph shows bone marrow.

A skeleton is strong and very light, because it is made from bone. Bone gets its strength by combining flexibility with stiffness. It gets its flexibility from tough, elastic fibers of a material called collagen, which thread through the bone. The stiffness comes from hard deposits of minerals, especially calcium and phosphates, which coat the collagen fibers. Without calcium and other minerals, bones would be rubbery. Without collagen fibers, they would be brittle and easy to break.

Bone is light because it is full of holes. Under the solid casing of the long bones of your limbs, for instance, is a tangle of thin rods called osteons. In the center of the bone is jellylike marrow, crisscrossed by delicate bony struts. The struts look fragile, but they provide a strong framework.

All the bones of the skeleton link together at joints. Nearly all joints are moveable. They are wrapped in fibers called ligaments, which hold the joints in place but allow them to move. How they move depends on the way the bones interlock. Most bones end in joints that are covered in smooth, rubbery cartilage. This protects the bones from wear and tear as they move against each other.

BODY POWER

Every move you make—running, jumping, scratching your nose—uses muscles. You even need muscles to sit still.

There are more than 600 muscles in the body, and they allow a huge range of movements. All muscles work by either contracting to pull two

A powerlift shows just how effective muscle power can be. This huge weight is lifted simply by the contraction of minute muscle fibers in the weightlifter's body.

In focus

KINDS OF MUSCLE

There are three kinds of muscle: skeletal, smooth, and cardiac. Skeletal muscles are the flesh of the body. These are the muscles that you control to help you move. Smooth muscles are found in tubelike organs, such as the digestive system. They contract to move things through the tube. Cardiac muscle is the special muscle that makes up the heart.

points together or by relaxing. Most muscles are attached to a bone on both sides of a joint, either directly or with a set of fibers called tendons.

Muscles are made up of long thin cells, or fibers. The fibers can contract (shorten) or relax (lengthen) over and over again. It is these fibers that give

In the real world

MUSCLE BUILDING
Some people are naturally strong, others are naturally weak. But everyone can build up strength through regular exercise. Exercise makes muscles bigger and stronger in two ways. When you first start to train, the exercise simply makes the muscle fibers fatter. But, as you train more, the muscle begins to grow new fibers. Exercise also builds up "cardiovascular" fitness, which is the heart and lung's ability to supply the oxygen that muscles need for fuel.

Bulging biceps—the muscles of the front upper arm—show how training can change the shape of the muscle.

muscles their power. Some muscles have just a few hundred fibers. Others contain more than 250,000 fibers.

Like string, muscle fibers are made up of tiny threads or striations. The striations are, in turn, made from strands of two different proteins—actin and myosin. The actin and myosin in the edges of each strand interlock like fingers. When your brain sends the muscle a signal to contract, little buds on each of millions of myosin fingers twist sharply. As they twist, they drag the actin filaments with them and so pull the muscle shorter.

BODY CONTROL

The human body is made up of lots of different systems. Two control mechanisms keep all the systems working together. These are the central nervous system and the chemical messengers called hormones.

Nerves are the body's hotlines—wirelike fibers that carry signals directly between the brain and the rest of the body. The focus of the nervous system is the central nervous system, or CNS. The CNS consists of the

Modern scanning techniques have enabled scientists to take special photographs inside people's heads to reveal a living brain in action.

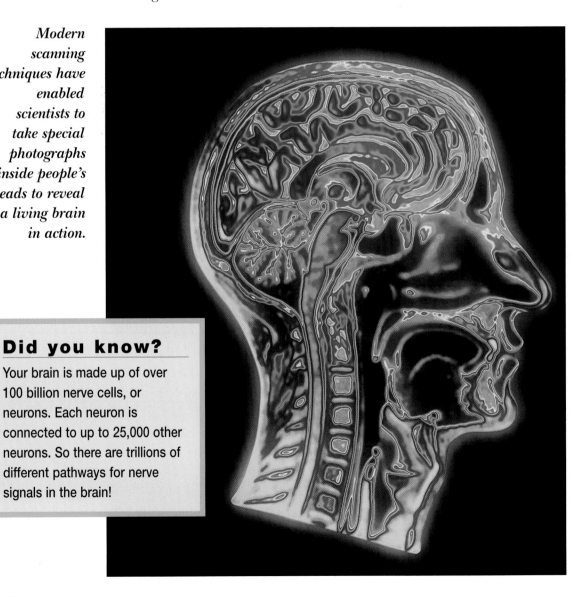

Did you know?

Your brain is made up of over 100 billion nerve cells, or neurons. Each neuron is connected to up to 25,000 other neurons. So there are trillions of different pathways for nerve signals in the brain!

TWO KINDS OF NERVES

There are two basic kinds of nerves—sensory nerves and motor nerves. Sensory nerves are nerves that take messages from the senses to the brain. Motor nerves are nerves that take messages from the brain telling the muscles to move. Each part of the body is linked to the brain by both sensory nerves and motor nerves. The two types run alongside each other, feeding back information and bringing instructions.

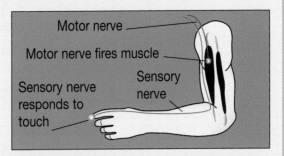

Motor nerve
Motor nerve fires muscle
Sensory nerve
Sensory nerve responds to touch
Sensory nerve

Sensory nerves feed back touch data from the fingers, and motor nerves control muscles to move your hand.

brain and the spinal cord—the bundle of nerves in your backbone. Every nerve signal starts or ends in the CNS.

Thousands of nerves spread out from the CNS to all parts of the body. These nerves make up the peripheral nervous system, or PNS. Nerve signals move through the PNS from the senses (eyes, ears, and so on) telling the brain what is going on around the body. Then, nerve signals pass back from the brain to the muscles, telling them what to do.

Hormones work in a different way. They are chemicals that have an effect on particular organs. Different organs respond only to certain hormones, so the effect is very specific. Hormones are released in small quantities from stores called glands. They travel through the bloodstream to their target. Hormones are slower than nerves, but longer lasting.

THE FIVE SENSES

Your body has five senses, to tell you what is going on in the world around you. They are sight, hearing, touch, smell, and taste. Sight comes through the eyes, two balls in your head that feed your brain pictures, rather like a video camera. A lens in the front focuses the picture onto a pattern of light-sensitive cells inside the back of the eyeball. The ears are incredibly sensitive mechanisms inside your head, arranged to respond to the minute vibrations in the air made by sounds. Touch comes from nerve endings all through your skin, which react to four kinds of feeling—a light touch, steady pressure, heat and cold, and pain. Smell relies on special cells inside your nose. Taste is a mixture of sensations, including smell, but your tongue also has special receptors to detect certain tastes.

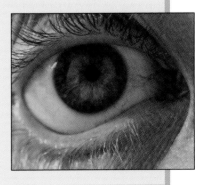

Light enters the eye through the dark pupil at the eye's center.

GROWING AND CHANGING

You will need

- A soft tape measure, such as a dressmaker's measure
- A ruler
- A pencil
- A notebook for keeping records

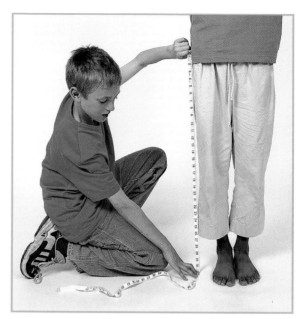

1 The first thing to measure is the length of your legs. Get a friend to measure you from waist to ground in bare feet.

What is happening?

From the moment you are conceived (the point where a sperm and egg fuse to make a new life) until you are in your late teens, your body grows bigger and bigger.
You grow fastest in your first few years, then grow more slowly, until a growth spurt in your early teenage years. Not every part of the body develops at the same rate. When a baby is born, its head is already three-quarters the size it is going to be in adulthood. By the time a child is one, its head is almost full adult size. The head appears to get smaller in relation to the rest of the body as a person grows older, while the legs and arms grow longer.

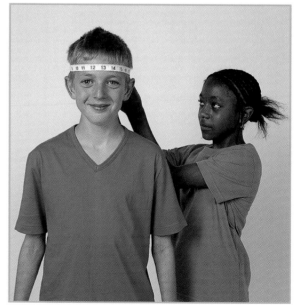

3 The third thing to measure is the size of your head. Measure the crown (around the top) and from neck to top.

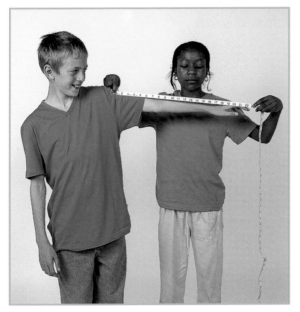

2 The second thing to measure is your arms. Measure from the bony point on your shoulder to your fingertips.

Finally measure your overall height. Tape the tape measure to a ruler. Then hold the ruler level on top of your head while your friend reads the measurement. Repeat the measurements at three-month intervals to see if bits of your body are growing at different rates. Each time you measure, divide the measurements for your legs, arms, and head, in turn, into the measurement for your height. If the divided figure is smaller than in the previous measurements, that part of your body is growing faster. If you can, make the same measurements of the head, legs, and arms of an infant and an adult, and see how they compare with their overall height.

Experiments in Science

Science is about knowledge: it is concerned with knowing and trying to understand the world around us. The word comes from the Latin word, *scire*, to know.

In the early 17th century, the great English thinker Francis Bacon suggested that the best way to learn about the world was not simply to think about it, but to go out and look for yourself—to make observations and try things out. Ever since then, scientists have tried to approach their work with a mixture of observation and experiment. Scientists insist that an idea or theory must be tested by observation and experiment before it is widely accepted.

All the experiments in this book have been tried before, and the theories behind them are widely accepted. But that is no reason why you should accept them. Once you have done all the experiments in this book, you will know that the ideas are true not because we have told you that they are but because you have seen for yourself.

All too often in science, there is an external factor interfering with the result that the scientist just has not thought of. Sometimes this can make the experiment seem to work when it has not, as well as making it fail. One scientist conducted lots of demonstrations to show that a clever horse called Hans could count things and tap out the answer with his hoof. The horse was indeed clever, but, later, it was found that rather than counting, he was getting clues from tiny unconscious movements of the scientist's eyebrows.

This is why it is very important when conducting experiments to be as rigorous as you possibly can. The more casual you are, the more "eyebrow factors" you will let in. There will always be some things that you cannot control. But the more precise you are, the less these are likely to affect the outcome.

What went wrong?

However careful you are, your experiments may not work. If so, you should try to find out where you went wrong. Then repeat the experiment until you are absolutely sure you are doing everything right. Scientists learn as much, if not more, from experiments that go wrong as those that succeed. In 1929, Scottish scientist Alexander Fleming discovered the first antibiotic drug, penicillin, when he noticed that a bacteria culture he was growing for an experiment had gone moldy—and that the mold seemed to kill the bacteria. A poor scientist would probably have thrown the moldy culture away. A good scientist is one who looks for alternative explanations for unexpected results.

Glossary

artery: A tubelike blood vessel that carries blood rich in oxygen away from the heart. Because the blood in arteries is rich in oxygen, it is bright red, unlike the blood in veins.

cardiovascular: Relating to the heart and blood vessels and the blood that circulates through them.

cartilage: A tough rubbery substance present in places in the body where bone would be too stiff—in the nose, for example, and in joints, to cushion the ends of bones.

central nervous system, or CNS: The nerves that make up the brain and the spinal cord. All nerves start and end here, and the CNS is the body's control center.

enzyme: A chemical substance needed to make some processes occur or speed them up. Digestion relies on enzymes that help break down the food.

hemoglobin: The oxygen-carrying chemical in red blood cells. It attracts oxygen when there is plenty of it and releases it when there is a shortage.

hormone: Chemicals released by glands in the body to make certain processes happen.

immune system: The body's array of defenses against microscopic invaders, such as germs. It includes physical barriers, such as the skin and mucus, and chemical weapons, such as white blood cells.

joint: Place in the body where two bones meet. Joints include the ankle, shoulder, and knee.

neuron: Nerve cell.

peripheral nervous system, or PNS: The nerves around the body that pass messages to and from the central nervous system.

protein: The basic chemical substances from which all living things are built up and on which they rely for many processes.

respiration: The chemical process by which food is broken down in cells, using oxygen to release energy. It is also another word for breathing.

spinal cord: The bundle of nerves running down through the backbone, from which all nerves radiate to the rest of the body.

vein: A tubelike blood vessel that carries blood from which the oxygen has been used back to the heart. The blood in veins is purplish in color because it is lacking in oxygen.

vitamins: Chemicals that you must have in your food in small quantities for various vital body processes.

Index